BCC PRESS

By Common Consent Press is a non-profit publisher dedicated to producing affordable, high-quality books that help define and shape the Latter-day Saint experience. BCC Press publishes books that address all aspects of Mormon life. Our mission includes finding manuscripts that will contribute to the lives of thoughtful Latter-day Saints, mentoring authors and nurturing projects to completion, and distributing important books to the Mormon audience at the lowest possible cost.

POEMS TOWARD ZION

TWO MASTERS

jared forsyth

For information contact
By Common Consent Press
972 East Burnham Lane
Draper, Utah 84020

Cover design: D Christian Harrison
Book design: Andrew Heiss

www.bccpress.org
ISBN-13: 978-1-961471-22-1

10 9 8 7 6 5 4 3 2 1

With this collection, Jared Forsyth offers up a thoughtful rendering of Christ's more provocative readings attuned to our day.
—Fiona Givens
coauthor of *The God Who Weeps*,
The Christ Who Heals, and *All Things New*

Jared Forsyth's *Two Masters* is an introspective collection full of wit, wisdom, and unsparing honesty. In simple language, he asks penetrating and sometimes uncomfortable questions drawn from scriptural teachings on money and wealth: What does it mean to prosper? Must generosity be deserved? Does self-reliance fit into Zion, where oneness of heart and mind are central? Each poem probes a different facet of the tension between spiritual ideals and assumed material realities. I highly recommend this thought-provoking book, especially if you enjoy exploring new ways to meaningfully apply ancient scripture in modern life
—Merrijane Rice
Author of *Messages on the Water*

Sometimes, we try to domesticate Jesus of Nazareth. We ask him to stand for whatever it is we already believe. If we're not careful, Jesus becomes a mascot, not a master.

But Jared Forsyth's had enough of reverent complacency. Using a poet's tools of imagery and irony, Jared is asking—really asking—what the scriptures have to say about our relationship with money. Page after page, these poems approach familiar stories from an unexpected angle. How would it feel to walk away from financial security like Laman and Lemuel? What prayer was in a money-changer's heart in the morning of that day when a strange preacher arrived and ruined everything?

Yes, Jared is opening doors that we usually leave safely shut when the Savior comes to visit our minds and hearts. And now Jesus is out and at it again, throwing over my tables.

—James Goldberg
author of *Let Me Drown with Moses* and
Tales of the Chelm First Ward

Contents

Who is this Jesus?

Alas, Babylon

Where can I turn for peace?

Dreams of a better way

Introduction

For several years now, economics has been at the forefront of my mind as I engage with scripture, and I've been struck with just how often money and finances are mentioned. The famous "pride cycle" in the Book of Mormon might be more aptly named the "wealth & inequality cycle" (2 Nephi 9:30; Helaman 3:36, 4:12, 6:17, 7:26, 13:21; Alma 4:6, 45:24; 3 Nephi 6:12; 4 Nephi 1:43), and the Doctrine and Covenants has some quite harsh things to say about those who don't share the earth's resources with the poor (56:16, 104:18, 105:3)—to name just a few examples.

And yet when we read these scriptures in church, all too often we skip over their implications—or even "wrest the scriptures" into a completely different meaning. This can happen for a variety of benign reasons; not wanting to make people uncomfortable, or not wanting a contentious issue to distract from some other point we want to emphasize.

A particularly egregious instance of this is what really kick-started my journey to writing this book of poetry. I was attending the opening night of the church's "self-reliance" program in our stake, and we read from the pamphlet a verse of scripture as a frame for the night's discussion, to underline the importance of self-reliance. "And it is my purpose to provide for my saints, for all things are mine. But it must needs be done in mine own way;" (D&C 104:15–16). The pamphlet then stated that the "Lord's way" for providing for the saints was self-reliance.

Opening the scriptures to section 104, I was surprised to find that they had actually stopped in the middle of a verse: the rest of verse 16 reads "and behold this is the way that I, the Lord, have decreed to provide for my saints, that the poor shall be exalted, in that the rich are made low." On reflection, maybe it's not surprising that they skipped over that part—it doesn't sound like self-reliance at all! In fact, it's not hard to read it as calling for radical wealth redistribution, which was tried a couple of times in the early church, but which would make many of us in our modern age very uncomfortable.

Ever since that occasion, I've been particularly sensitized to the ways that scripture talks about money and financial matters, and especially the ways in which, if we took them seriously, they'd call us to make some quite uncomfortable changes. This is what I've tried to do with these poems: really take Jesus seriously, asking the question "what if I read this, not as metaphor or parable, but as actual concrete advice?"

Many of my favorite images from scripture have to do with the beloved community called Zion. Alma exhorts his little flock to have their "hearts knit together in unity and in love one towards another" (Mosiah 18:21), and of the city of Enoch we read: "the Lord called his people Zion, because they were of one heart and one mind, and dwelt in righteousness; and there was no poor among them" (Moses 7:18). My heart longs for such a community! And it seems clear to me that one of the many barriers between us and Zion is an economic one. We live in a society with vast (and growing) disparity between the rich and the poor, where at every hand we are encouraged to devote our heart, might, mind and strength to the accrual of wealth, where scarcity dominates so many of our thoughts and interactions with others, and relationships are increasingly commodified and instrumentalized. How can we hope to fight such a tide? As with many issues of the soul, I believe it starts with the practice of paying attention.

One of the things I love about poetry—and literature in general—is its ability to help us approach discomfort from an oblique angle, where we might shy away if taken head-on. The best poems that I've read, like the best scriptures, have become companions for me, sparking conversation after conversation, prompting me to new insights and engagement with my life and with difficult topics.

That, more than anything, is my hope for this book of poetry; that these poems will be a spark for you in discussions with friends and family, encouraging us all to do the slow hard work of making a world where we can all thrive, having our "hearts knit together in unity and love," where none need fear loneliness or deprivation.

—Jared Forsyth

Acknowledgments

I would like to thank my wonderful wife Selina for the conversations which sparked many of these poems, and for contributing two of her own excellent poems to this collection; my father, Jon Forsyth, for the artwork that sets the tone for each section of poems; James Goldberg for his mentorship and editing feedback, without which many of these poems would be much diminished; Holly Kolb for her editing feedback, and the whole BCC Press team for shepherding this work into the world. This book was kickstarted by the Mormon Lit Lab book mentorship program, and wouldn't have been possible without their guidance and support.

Who is this Jesus?

Mortgage

I mortgaged my soul
for a share of the world
and I'm paying it off
despite a high rate
of variable interest

The returns of the world-share
are way beyond my expectations
and soon I'll refinance
to increase my stake

A salesman came knocking
said "we buy souls—in any condition"
I was a little offended
What kind of condition did he think my soul was in?

He wouldn't tell me the offer price
Typical salesman
tried to feed me some line about "money not being involved"
kept going on about bread, and fountains
milk and honey

As if the bank would be satisfied with stories.

The public defender

The public defender
assigned to me
doesn't seem to be trying very hard

this lawsuit is clearly ridiculous
fantastic
no way they could prove wrongdoing
and for what? a coat?

and this lawyer
can you believe it?
trying to get me
to take a plea deal
that he proposed!
give up the coat
without a fight
throw in the cloak
for good measure

Scam

it's definitely a scam

the supposed inheritance
(from a long lost relative
who left a cryptic will)
is a dead giveaway
"a kingdom"
do those even exist anymore?
and who would want *me*
to rule over anything?

and the transfer fee
(that's how they get you)
isn't a fixed sum,
but a percentage of my income

and what kind of swindler
includes behavioral stipulations?
changing my lifestyle
my habits and motivations
caring for the poor
seeking justice and wisdom

it's got to be a scam

Leaving

"We won't need any money where we're going"

that sounds like a threat
that sounds like scavenging
hard labor, subsistence living
either that
or a death cult

which, given the way dad's been acting
isn't entirely out of the question

why leave it behind?
surely wherever we end up
there will be people who like shiny things
and want to give us, in return
the life of comfort
we deserve

this is our inheritance,
this is our future,
this is our hope you're throwing away
based on what, a premonition?

had a bad dream
and you want to leave
all of these
precious

things

Worry

If we weary the Lord
enough with our asking
will he let us
worry
about money

The money-changer's prayer, part 1

O God
I thank thee
that thou has been so good to me
the windows of heaven
clear evidence of your favor

it's an honor
to be in your holy house
the first to touch these sacrifices
fetching whatever price
the market will bear

please grant me
continued stability
safety for my wares
and a fruitful passover

The money-changer's prayer, part 2

O God,
where art thou in mine extremity?
wherefore hast thou turned thy face from me
and allowed this great misfortune to befall me?

I look for comfort, and behold, negligence;
I look for safety, and my life is upturned.

How long wilt thou suffer my noble work to be disrupted
and derided by these outside agitators?

Union

We've caught wind that the boss has been offering
much higher wages to more recent hires
while those of us who have worked here the longest
haven't seen the slightest hint of a raise

So we're trying to form a union
Equal pay for equal work
He can't keep playing with us like this
"do what he wants with his money" indeed

Summer Home

My summer home
in Babylon
is full of beggars

some homeless vagrant
broke in while I was away
invited all his friends,
set up a soup kitchen
and a field hospital
planted a community garden
converted the ballroom
to a dormitory
and the study
to a sanctuary

I was going to bring my in-laws
for a weekend stay in the city
attend a few charity dinners
see the sights
as one does
attempt again, in vain of course
to convince old acquaintances
to flee Babylon
and come to Zion

get away from the filth
the crass
the appalling

and shelter with us
where it's safe

Rich

Matthew 21:28–32

The rich young man
who went away
and didn't follow Christ

thereafter had
a change of heart
renounced his goods,
lived life with want.

When I was asked
to pledge my means
I said "yes," as expected

but given that I have them still,
who did the father's will?

Treasure

I hid my treasure in a mountain
because I wanted my heart
protected
but the mountain was made low

I hid my treasure in a rock
to protect my heart
from pain
but the rock was rent asunder

I hid my treasure in a city
to protect my heart
from loneliness
but the city was laid waste

I hid my treasure in the earth
to protect my heart
from thieves
but then I could not find it

Alas, Babylon

Seek

Oh, I did my time
seeking after the kingdom
from the sea to the sea
from the north to the east
such a thirst! such a search!
seeking God
and his righteousness

These days I've got riches
and I seek still more
for the best of intents,
you understand
Clothing and feeding,
liberating and such like

And the kingdom?
Well I guess
I must have found it
in some way
because, look around!
Success speaks for itself

Lower lights

In a storm like this, any extra light is a Godsend.

Of course, these days sailors don't have to rely on God's caprice.

Just download the LowerLite™ app, charge it up with funds, and in under a minute you'll be paired with a Lighter™ on the shore, holding a lantern only you can see.

Now just one lamp on the shore doesn't sound like much, and it isn't—you can up your bid to get up to 500 Lighters™ shining exclusively for you.

It's been nice for us on the shore, too. Now that Walmart moved in, sailors mostly ignore the little shops and open air market when they come into port. So signing up to be a Lighter™ can give us some much-needed extra cash.

I've been doing it for a couple months now, and for once I'm grateful to live on the most storm ridden length of coast in New England.

When there are multiple ships out there, they inevitably enter a bidding war, as each wants to access as many lights as possible—those are the really good nights.

And most nights, each ship manages to pick up enough lights not to crash.

Word of advice

"Don't cast pearls before swine"
so I keep my predictions
close to my chest

"pray to the Father in secret,
and he shall reward thee openly"
you can see for yourself that he has

"take no thought for the morrow
sufficient unto the day is the evil thereof"
that's why my trades
are minute-by-minute

They say the god of this trading floor
will eat you alive

But I know how
to be in the market
and not of the market

We are free

And Cain gloried in that which he had done, saying: I am free; surely
the flocks of my brother falleth into my hands.
—*Moses 5:33*

". . . we should have such an empire for liberty as she has never
surveyed since the creation"
—*Thomas Jefferson*

"Freedom" they said as they drove out the natives
"Freedom" they said as they razed ancient trees
Blood cries from the ground, but we are no one's keeper.
Surely we have become as our eldest brother:
We are free; the lands of our brothers have fallen into our hands.

Heavenly Home Equity Loans, Ltd.

Would you like to make use
of the equity you've been building
in that mansion
in that kingdom
up on high?

It'd be a shame
to let an asset like that sit dormant
instead of getting a head start
on enjoying the luxury
you've so painstakingly earned.

With a 60% loan, just think what you could do:
satisfy out-of-reach desires;
make evident your divine favor;
extend your influence far beyond your dreams!

Our rates are quite reasonable
and rising home values
are sure to much more than cover
the interest.

So, what do you say:
want to have your own
little bit of heaven
right away?

—John Doe, HHEL Senior Sales Rep

Money is no object

I assure you
money is no
object
indeed
it is the subject

I'm sorry to inform you
you are the object
here

Mint and anise and cumin

When tithing
becomes a status symbol
instead of a sacrifice

When obedience
becomes a status symbol
instead of a sacrifice

When sacrifice
becomes a status symbol
instead of a sacrifice

the altar of the Lamb
will never compete
with the altar
of your brother's esteem

Foolish virgins

After Merrijane Rice, "The Other Virgin"

Parables
worn smooth with time
and tongues and thoughts
slide easily
into familiar courses

The unjust judge
catches
like a newly missing tooth
Is God unjust?
Does God somehow
delight to see us beg?
or wait until
we have worn ourselves out
with asking?

The foolish virgins
should have known
that their wiser companions
were not kind
unready to sacrifice
if it meant their chance was jeopardized
they did not believe
that the God who fed a widow
from a drop of oil
could make theirs be
enough.

Increase

A man went on a journey, leaving his slaves with
two million dollars
one million dollars
and five hundred thousand dollars, respectively

The first went into real estate,
got a sweet deal on a development loan
leveraged a series of high-end rentals
in an up-and-coming part of town
and at the return of the master, had made a striking 100% profit.

The second took his lesser capital to commodities trading
and, making some big bets in emerging markets—
lithium in Bolivia, soy beans in Brazil—
grew his portfolio leaps and bounds,
and had also doubled his investment
when the master returned.

The third searched far and wide,
scoured the stock markets
interviewed financial experts
desperate for a means of market participation

that didn't hinge on extracting wealth
from those who had little to start with.

But at every turn, he saw

> to all those who have, more will be given, and they will have
> an abundance;
> but from those who have nothing, even what they have is
> given to another

and in despair, he fled to the woods,
and buried his weapons
of wealth in the ground.

Snake in the garden

There's a snake
in the garden
and he keeps going on
about futures

I've tried to tell him
we don't even have currency here
but he says
he can work with that

just imagine
he says
what a little bit of
free
market
could do for you

reduce risk
reward thrift
increase liquidity
drive down
margins

I'm used to it
and really
he must be awfully bored
now that we've established Zion

Self-reliance

The crime
of self-reliance
has many victims

The self
starved of the push
and pull
of other souls

The community
one interdependent member
poorer

The Christ within us
deprived both
of serving
and being served

For cursed is the one
that putteth their trust
in the arm of flesh.

Where can I
turn for peace?

Luke 16:1-12

I find myself
a steward of the Lord's funds,
and I'm about to lose my job.

It might be very soon,
the way the stock market's looking,
or it may take me
a few dozen years.

But the good book says
to trade this money for friends
to cancel others' debts

and break every yoke.

Wanted: someone who deserves this coat

Someone asked me for my coat today
I didn't give it to them

I couldn't be sure they deserved it

but
I'm not sure I deserve it
and my cloak is plenty warm

so
if you deserve this coat
you can have it

please bring adequate proof

Homework #5-40

How do you respond when someone asks for your coat?

_____

_____

_____

Do they deserve it? [y/n]

Do you deserve it? [y/n]

Does anyone deserve this coat? [y/n]

And if not, to whom is it to be given? _____

And to whom do you give the cloak also?

_____

_____

_____

Real

How real
is a penny
to a widow with only two?

How real
is a twenty
to a man eighty-seven away
from eviction

if eighty-seven dollars vanished
from my savings account

if eight hundred vanished
from my 401k

it would leave
my reality
undisturbed

Lost

See, if God had ten coins
or sheep
or kids
and then, lost one of them
dropped behind a couch, or rolled under the fridge
do you think God would just, forget about it?
in the face of eternity,
endless progeny,
what's one more kid.
Would God just take the loss?
No!
God would search everywhere
find the person
vacuum off the dust bunnies
and then throw a party
and maybe cry a little.

A Toast

Luke 12:16–21

A toast, I say
to our recently departed
benefactor
let no one say
he did not bring forth plentifully
such plenty that we now enjoy

if only he could see
the good his goods are doing
for at the time of his demise
there was no will, or heir
nor even a place to store the bounty
(the barns having just been torn down)
and, lacking other options,
it has now fallen to us

may God smile upon him
for his posthumous generosity

The Sown

And the cares of this world, and the deceitfulness of riches, and the lusts of other things entering in, choke the word, and it becometh unfruitful.
—Mark 4:18–19

the cares of this world
yes, I see them
too many to number
and even the slightest
relentless enough to drown in

the deceitfulness of riches
oh, I could go on and on.
a tool, a trap, a culture,
a whole way of life.

the lusts of other things
to be liked. to be safe.
to be right. to be great.

as I sit in this ditch
I wonder

I did not sow these thorns
neither did I cast myself among them

should I, then, pray
for cleansing flames?

Tuberculosis

The world is full of miserable places. One way of living comfortably is not to think about them or, when you do, to send money.
—Mountains Beyond Mountains *by Tracy Kidder*

I don't want to think about
the suffering of millions
from tuberculosis
I don't feel smart enough
to come up with a plan to fix it
What if
God has already thought about this
and has a perfect plan for fixing it

I've tried asking God
what the plan is to fix it
but I'm not getting anywhere
What if
Sharon Eubank has already asked God
what the plan is to fix it
and LDS Charities is implementing
that perfect plan
I'm so glad
I don't have to think about it
anymore.

Lend

Instead, love your enemies, do good, and lend, expecting nothing in return. Your reward will be great.
—Luke 6:35

The Anointed One
doesn't seem to care
that if I keep lending
without expecting the money back
I'll run out fast.

Of course, if I could multiply dollars like loaves and fishes
or turn water into crude oil
pass it around the neighborhood
and return with more than we started . . .

. . . but come to think of it
for all his talk of money
has he ever actually touched it?
Peter paid his taxes
with the coin from the fish.
He turned tables in the temple
without the lucre ever soiling his palms
"The coin of Rome, who's face is on it?"
Almost like he had to be reminded.

Don't get me wrong, I love the guy, and honestly
I wish I could be so unstained
but I've got short-term liabilities
and only long-term assets
I'm just trying to keep my cash flow positive
as I await that eternal reward.

Christmas texts

Christmas time
and the text messages
from desperate folks
in the mutual aid group
we joined at the start of the pandemic
start coming in

We pay someone's overdue heating bill,
equivalent to 8 months of our own;
give someone else the cash
to pay for gas
to keep their car running
in the hotel parking lot,
refer them to a women's shelter
to get help finding stability

tell me, master,
what good thing must I do,
that these might be saved?

Tornado

A tornado tore through
the Amazon warehouse
not too far from here
six people, dead
just trying to put
bread on the table
working unforgiving hours
under invasive scrutiny

just so some of us can enjoy
the good things in life
a little sooner

I was idling, that windy evening,
on my couch, in my basement,
my workday none too strenuous
and long since finished
enjoying an evening's leisure

and two days later
we *still* received our package

I apparently do own stock
in Amazon, though indirectly
through an index fund
whose governing principle

is to only invest in stocks
that are "socially good"

the return has been excellent
gaining 50% in these two pandemic years
as order volumes increased dramatically
and wages didn't

and I try in vain
to wash the stain
of the laborer's bread
from my idle hands

Build

If I could build Zion
by burning what isn't
I'd light a match right now

Eyes to see

My dear sisters and brothers, you too can pray for the Lord to open your eyes to see things you would not normally see. Even in our busy lives, we can follow the example of Jesus and see individuals—their needs, their faith, their struggle, and who they can become.
—Michelle D. Craig, October 2020 General Conference

My eyes
skitter off the people
on the median
and their cardboard signs

"just lost my husband"
"please help my kid"
"god bless"

My hands
go to the glovebox
and the bills I keep around,
solely for this purpose
did I remember to get cash-back
on my last grocery run?

"down on my luck"
though it's hard to conceive
of the luck I'd have to suffer
to end up in their shoes

My thoughts
immediately turn to systems
institutions
the compound failures of humanity
and community
that leaves this ever-changing cast
of desperates
pacing the solid white line
between stopped cars

Somebody really ought to do something

Scarcity

By Selina Forsyth

What if
Scarcity
spreads
like a virus?

Then I will stay in my own circles;
Quarantine those who have it—
or are likely to get it—
as far from myself as possible.

But God says,
"the earth is full, and there is enough and to spare,"
If scarcity and abundance are shared.

What if
Love
is my spirit's
immune response?

Dreams of a better way

Nostalgia

Wherefore, the prophets, and the priests, and the teachers, did labor diligently, persuading them to look forward unto the Messiah, and believe in him to come as though he already was.
—Jarom 1:11

If Zion's streets were threatened:
the joyful order marred
by the slow death of class division
or the quick death of cataclysm

what effort would we not spare
to preserve that precious
way of life?

but
instead we're here,
in not-yet-Zion
with shopping lists,
and after-school programs,
the homeless man by the playground,
the friend with a messy divorce,
wars, and rumors of wars
as long as I've been alive

and, wouldn't it be nice
if we could all come together
and build something better?

can we, somehow, cultivate a nostalgia
for the Zion we have yet to see?

Without them

What profit a man if he save his soul but lose the (natural) world?
—Lature

You without them
cannot be made perfect
the mice
the lichen
the aspens

The earth is enough and to spare
but will we spare the earth?

Scorched fields of empty chairs
species driven to and fro
as we secure fortunes
on earth and in heaven

Can we ignore the plight of the living world
as we sprint up the stairway to heaven?

When shall the earth rest?

Homeostasis

In some sense, bodies exist to exist.

Life is that which propagates itself
in ongoing defiance against entropy,
as though just continuing
is sufficient victory.

And yet something in us calls
for more than mere sustenance.

Does the body of Christ
exist for itself,
alone?

Dream Journal, p. 82

partial transcription

hello?
yes this is smith & marx
consulting group
we couldn't help but notice
you're trying to build a good society
free of poverty, exploitation, distress
and
we have some thoughts
no, we really don't have time
for questions
you'll be woken up in a few minutes
your dog barking I believe
and we have a strict
one-dream-per-dreamer policy
so many to get to, you understand
anyway
you see we've had a long time to think about our mistakes
and of course others mistakes
we thought all it would take
is for enough people of pure intent
and love of community
to get together
but it turns out, you need to-
[unreadable]

The Higher Law

You have heard it said
by them of old time
"thou shalt not covet"
but I say unto you,
"thou shalt not covet
thine own property." (D&C 19:26)

You have heard it said
by them of old time
"thou shalt not steal"
But behold I say unto you
"if any man shall take
of the abundance which I have made,
and impart not his portion
unto the poor and the needy,
he shall, with the wicked,
lift up his eyes in hell." (D&C 104:18)

You have heard it said
by them of old time
"You shall have no other gods before Me"
but I say unto you
"No man can serve two masters . . .
Ye cannot serve God and Mammon." (Matthew 6:24)

Financial Laws of Zion

The first financial law of Zion
is "live within our means"
—*our*, not your—
for, with a mighty hand
the Lord God Almighty
brought us, not just you, out of Egypt.

The second financial law of Zion:
"the laborer is worthy of their hire"
whether you arrange with the bishop
to work one hour or ten
at carpentry or poetry
your reward is fellowship
and abundance.

The third financial law of Zion:
"the earth is full
with enough and to spare"
—if we do not,
like wicked husbandman,
burn the forests
and cause children
to pass through the fire.

And the poor

I'm trying to build Zion
and the poor keep coming in

I'm setting up covenants
establishing boundaries
and the poor keep coming in

I'm gathering funding
organizing food storage
raising houses and barns
and the poor keep coming in

we're electing a council
and the poor keep coming in
the poor keep coming in
the poor keep coming in

Menial

Fully-automated
luxury communism
would have us all live
like royalty
a Zion, of sorts, for all would be rich
no need to foist our unpleasant tasks
onto a lower-class
of people
Automation would, somehow
provide all the care,
provide for all needs,
provide all for all.

Was there no poop in the garden?
no latrines to clean?

When a King
stands up
and presents himself
a beggar before God
boasts of working with his hands
with his sweat

When a King
comes down
as a beggar
without home or bed
and sweats
blood

I think that Zion
may be hard.

Respect

Poverty, says Smith*,
is the lack of those things necessary
to live a respectable life.

In Zion, are there none un-equal?
Or do they simply give all
respect?

---

*Adam Smith

This House

Let this house
be a house of poverty
a house of mourning
a house of meekness
a house of hunger and thirst
a house of mercy
a house of integrity
a house of peace
a house of the persecuted,
and the reviled.

Beggar

And thou shalt take no purse nor scrip, neither staves, neither two coats, for the church shall give unto thee in the very hour what thou needest for food and for raiment, and for shoes and for money, and for scrip.
—D&C 24:18

Do you have the courage,
missionary,
to depend wholly
for your substance
on the flock you go to tend?

Do you have the faith
in their charity
and mercy
to come as a beggar seeking alms?

For the teacher is not above the hearer
and the first shall be last

What kind of Zion are you waiting for
before you cast yourself upon it?

Need

I was taught to say I have no need of thee
as a youth, as a teen, and adult.
You do as you will, and it won't impact me
for I have no need of thee.

So I settle all debts and protect against ties
my burdens are light and my own
I stride on through life until I realize
at the end I am lonely, alone.

The world and its burdens could also be mine
if I stop and I sit here with you.
the sick, the imprisoned, the stranger outside
and they carry my burdens too.

So teach me to say I have need of thee
to each one who crosses my path.
Your fate and mine, they must be entwined
for I do have need of thee.

Enough

By Selina Forsyth

D&C 104:17–18; Ether 12:23–27

Enough
sounds like a sigh
like the tension flowing out
of muscles and minds
hearts
and stomachs

while I struggle to grasp
that the earth is Enough
for all gnawing bellies
and grace is Enough
for my clenched hands

the very air
whispers
Enough
is the substance
of grace

faith is the inhale
—gasping, sometimes—
of God's
Enough

God
grant me the
grace
to exhale

Author's Notes

Who is this Jesus? (p. 1)

Mortgage (p. 3)

I love the way this combines the financialization of everyday life (where corporations are increasingly interested in getting individuals onto payment plans, and the public are encouraged to get involved with more and more complicated financial instruments) with the really poignant scriptures about losing our souls. In our sophisticated day and age, there's no need to actually sell your soul—just put it up as collateral!

Referenced scriptures:

2 Nephi 26:25
   25 Behold, doth he cry unto any, saying: Depart from me? Behold, I say unto you, Nay; but he saith: Come unto me all ye ends of the earth, buy milk and honey, without money and without price.

3 Nephi 20:38
   38 For thus saith the Lord: Ye have sold yourselves for naught, and ye shall be redeemed without money.

Matthew 16:25

> [25] For what profit is it to a man if he gains the whole world, and loses his own soul? Or what will a man give in exchange for his soul?

Isaiah 55:1

> [1] Ho, every one that thirsteth, come ye to the waters, and he that hath no money; come ye, buy, and eat; yea, come, buy wine and milk without money and without price.

The public defender (p. 4)

In the United States court system, those who are "indigent" and unable to hire a lawyer to represent them are to be provided with a "public defender." Here I've put Jesus in the role of public defender, but as he warns us in Matthew, we might not like his style of litigation. Be careful what you beg for.

Christ is sometimes called our "Advocate with the father," calling to mind "penal substitution" theories of atonement, but here we're thinking about Christ being our (counter) advocate in conflicts with our fellow humans.

It's remarkable how misaligned Christ's advice to "love your enemies" is with our current systems of criminal and civil justice.

Referenced scriptures:

Matthew 5:38–42

> [38] Ye have heard that it hath been said, An eye for an eye, and a tooth for a tooth: [39] But I say unto you, That ye resist not evil: but whosoever shall smite thee on thy right cheek, turn to him the other also. [40] And if any man will sue thee at the law, and take away thy coat, let him have thy cloak also. [41] And whosoever shall compel thee to go a mile, go with him twain. [42] Give to him that asketh thee, and from him that would borrow of thee turn not thou away.

D&C 29:5

> [5] Lift up your hearts and be glad, for I am in your midst, and am your advocate with the Father; and it is his good will to give you the kingdom.

D&C 110:4

> [4] I am the first and the last; I am he who liveth, I am he who was slain; I am your advocate with the Father.

Mosiah 4:19–20

> [19] For behold, are we not all beggars? Do we not all depend upon the same Being, even God, for all the substance which we have, for both food and raiment, and for gold, and for silver, and for all the riches which we have of every kind? [20] And behold, even at this time, ye have been calling on his name, and begging for a remission of your sins. And has he suffered that ye have begged in vain?

Scam (p. 5)

Of all of the categories of spam swindle attempts common to our digital age, the so-called "Nigerian prince" scam has remarkable narrative appeal. The idea that there's someone out there with fantastic sums of money who is nevertheless barred from accessing it by tedious bureaucratic regulations, and you! the proud owner of both a social security number and a bank account, will be the one to provide aid in this time of critical need.

The Christian promise of a heavenly kingdom almost has a similar feel to it, and I couldn't help but make the comparison. How many of Jesus's teachings, if encountered today, would come across as ravings or the work of a conman?

Referenced scriptures:

Matthew 6:19–21

> [19] Lay not up for yourselves treasures upon earth, where moth and rust doth corrupt, and where thieves break through and steal: [20] But lay up for yourselves treasures in heaven, where neither moth nor rust doth corrupt, and where thieves do not break through nor steal: [21] For where your treasure is, there your heart will be also.

Matthew 25:34

> [34] Then shall the King say unto them on his right hand, Come, ye blessed of my Father, inherit the kingdom prepared for you from the foundation of the world.

Micah 6:8

> ^{8} He hath shewed thee, O man, what is good; and what doth the LORD require of thee, but to do justly, and to love mercy, and to walk humbly with thy God?

Leaving (p. 6)

Money is so thoroughly enmeshed in our relationship with the world that it can be terrifying to contemplate going entirely without it. And yet that seems to be, in many instances, what Jesus is calling us to!

I appreciate recent attempts in fiction to cast Laman and Lemuel as more sympathetic figures; folks who have an arguably rational response to some of the extreme circumstances they encounter.

Referenced scriptures:

1 Nephi 2:4

> ^{4} And it came to pass that [Lehi] departed into the wilderness. And he left his house, and the land of his inheritance, and his gold, and his silver, and his precious things, and took nothing with him, save it were his family, and provisions, and tents, and departed into the wilderness.

1 Nephi 2:11

> ^{11} Now this he spake because of the stiffneckedness of Laman and Lemuel; for behold they did murmur in many things against their father, because he was a visionary man, and had led them out of the land of Jerusalem, to leave the land of their inheritance, and their gold, and their silver, and their precious things, to perish in the wilderness. And this they said he had done because of the foolish imaginations of his heart.

Worry (p. 7)

Reading through the New Testament, I imagine a conversation where we keep coming back to Jesus, saying "but can we please worry about money?" and he just keeps saying "no."

Referenced scriptures:

Luke 18:1–5

[1] And he spake a parable unto them to this end, that men ought always to pray, and not to faint; [2] Saying, There was in a city a judge, which feared not God, neither regarded man: [3] And there was a widow in that city; and she came unto him, saying, Avenge me of mine adversary. [4] And he would not for a while: but afterward he said within himself, Though I fear not God, nor regard man; [5] Yet because this widow troubleth me, I will avenge her, lest by her continual coming she weary me.

Matthew 6:25–33

[25] Therefore I say unto you, Take no thought for your life, what ye shall eat, or what ye shall drink; nor yet for your body, what ye shall put on. Is not the life more than meat, and the body than raiment? [26] Behold the fowls of the air: for they sow not, neither do they reap, nor gather into barns; yet your heavenly Father feedeth them. Are ye not much better than they? [27] Which of you by taking thought can add one cubit unto his stature? [28] And why take ye thought for raiment? Consider the lilies of the field, how they grow; they toil not, neither do they spin: [29] And yet I say unto you, That even Solomon in all his glory was not arrayed like one of these. [30] Wherefore, if God so clothe the grass of the field, which to day is, and to morrow is cast into the oven, shall he not much more clothe you, O ye of little faith? [31] Therefore take no thought, saying, What shall we eat? or, What shall we drink? or, Wherewithal shall we be clothed? [32] (For after all these things do the Gentiles seek:) for your heavenly Father knoweth that ye have need of all these things. [33] But seek ye first the kingdom of God, and his righteousness; and all these things shall be added unto you.

The money-changer's prayer, part 1 (p. 8)

This poem was inspired in large part by a clip that I came across from "The Ramsey Show" entitled "Should Landlords Feel Guilty About Raising Rent Prices?" On it, Dave Ramsey, the famous Christian Money Guru, answers a question from a landlord in an area where rental rates are rising quickly, who is worried that raising their rents to match the market will displace renters.

Dave's answer is immediate and unequivocal. He denies any element of tension, saying simply: "You didn't displace that person, the housing market did. You didn't cause inflation," and finally "the bible doesn't require us to under-charge."

I wonder how he interprets Christ's injunction in Luke to "lend, expecting nothing in return" (Luke 6:35).

It really seems like Dave is declaring that "following the Market" is unquestionably moral—either that, or that there is simply no moral valence to pricing decisions for necessary goods and services. Wherever he's coming from, I find it baffling.

Of course, it is so much simpler to just decide there's no moral component, that there's nothing to be agonized over, as the alternative is to reckon with the deep unmet needs and rampant tragedies that pervade our modern economic landscape. If you can convince yourself that you don't have a duty or obligation to use your means to provide for those with less, then it becomes far easier to make "prudent economic decisions."

I have friends and relatives who use real estate as a financial investment (owning a condo to rent out to college students, for example), but whenever I've considered working toward that myself, I am stymied by the prospect of making decisions such as the one posed by the caller to the Dave Ramsey show, where moral action seems infeasible, or at least beyond my ability to determine.

The money-changer's prayer, part 2 (p. 9)

This is of course imagining one of the "money changers" that were cast out of the temple during Jesus's famous table-flipping episode. It is too easy, when considering the people that opposed Jesus in the New Testament, to cast them all as cynical hypocrites, without real devotion or faith. But I think it's far more likely that many or even most of them were quite devoted according to their own traditions and practices, and that they prayed and expected God's favor just as much as you or I.

Referenced scriptures:

Isaiah 5:7
> [7] For the vineyard of the LORD of hosts is the house of Israel, and the men of Judah his pleasant plant: and he looked for judgment, but behold oppression; for righteousness, but behold a cry.

Habakkuk 1:2
> [2] O LORD, how long shall I cry, and thou wilt not hear! Even cry out unto thee of violence, and thou wilt not save!

Union (p. 10)

The parable of the laborers is deeply unfair by any standard of fairness that we're used to, and the householder in the parable is apparently doing this on purpose. If he had started out paying the first what was agreed, they likely would have gone on their way and not witnessed the "injustice," but because the "last were first," they expected that their wages would be changed from what was agreed.

This poem imagines turning a tool generally used by workers to rectify unjust working conditions against the one who, according to our theology, is "the most just."

Referenced scriptures:

Matthew 20:1–16
> [1] For the kingdom of heaven is like unto a man that is an householder, which went out early in the morning to hire labourers into his vineyard. [2] And when he had agreed with the labourers for a penny a day, he sent them into his vineyard. [3] And he went out about the third hour, and saw others standing idle in the marketplace, [4] And said unto them; Go ye also into the vineyard, and whatsoever is right I will give you. And they went their way. [5] Again he went out about the sixth and ninth hour, and did likewise. [6] And about the eleventh hour he went out, and found others standing idle, and saith unto them, Why stand ye here all the day idle? [7] They say unto him, Because no man hath hired us. He saith unto them, Go ye also into the vineyard; and whatsoever is right, that shall ye receive. [8] So

when even was come, the lord of the vineyard saith unto his steward, Call the labourers, and give them their hire, beginning from the last unto the first. [9] And when they came that were hired about the eleventh hour, they received every man a penny. [10] But when the first came, they supposed that they should have received more; and they likewise received every man a penny. [11] And when they had received it, they murmured against the goodman of the house, [12] Saying, These last have wrought but one hour, and thou hast made them equal unto us, which have borne the burden and heat of the day. [13] But he answered one of them, and said, Friend, I do thee no wrong: didst not thou agree with me for a penny? [14] Take that thine is, and go thy way: I will give unto this last, even as unto thee. [15] Is it not lawful for me to do what I will with mine own? Is thine eye evil, because I am good? [16] So the last shall be first, and the first last: for many be called, but few chosen.

Summer Home (p. 11)

The following image keeps showing up in General Conferences talks, ensign articles, and church manuals:

> To come to Zion, it is not enough for you or me to be somewhat less wicked than others. We are to become not only good but holy men and women. Recalling Elder Neal A. Maxwell's phrase, let us once and for all establish our residence in Zion and give up the summer cottage in Babylon (see Neal A. Maxwell, *A Wonderful Flood of Light* [1990], 47).
> —D. Todd Christofferson, "Come to Zion," October 2008

In the first place, it follows a very common theme in our absolutist religious culture, that any amount of "taint" or "exposure" is enough to be dangerously compromising. In the second, it both draws on and reinforces the "us vs them" narrative, where the world is separable into the holy and the unholy, with the injunction to cling to the one and shun the other.

I imagine Jesus, in our current age, would spend quite a bit of time in what we call Babylon, in the midst of the outcasts, proclaiming that the Kingdom of Heaven is among them already.

The image is also just a little funny to me, as you have to be pretty rich to have a summer cottage anywhere.

Rich (p. 12)

In the temple endowment, the final covenant is a pledge of all our time, talents, and earthly means, toward the building up of the Kingdom of God on the Earth, and the establishment of Zion. I've made that covenant, and yet there are many people of other faiths that are much closer to keeping it than I.

Referenced scriptures:

Matthew 19:16–22 (NIV)
> [16] Just then a man came up to Jesus and asked, "Teacher, what good thing must I do to get eternal life?" [17] "Why do you ask me about what is good?" Jesus replied. "There is only One who is good. If you want to enter life, keep the commandments." [18] "Which ones?" he inquired. Jesus replied, "'You shall not murder, you shall not commit adultery, you shall not steal, you shall not give false testimony, [19] honor your father and mother,' and 'love your neighbor as yourself.'" [20] "All these I have kept," the young man said. "What do I still lack?" [21] Jesus answered, "If you want to be perfect, go, sell your possessions and give to the poor, and you will have treasure in heaven. Then come, follow me." [22] When the young man heard this, he went away sad, because he had great wealth.

Matthew 21:28–32 (NRSV)
> [28] "What do you think? A man had two sons; he went to the first and said, 'Son, go and work in the vineyard today.' [29] He answered, 'I will not,' but later he changed his mind and went. [30] The father went to the second and said the same, and he answered, 'I go, sir,' but he did not go. [31] Which of the two did the will of his father?" They said, "The first." Jesus said to them, "Truly I tell you, the tax

collectors and the prostitutes are going into the kingdom of God ahead of you. [32] For John came to you in the way of righteousness, and you did not believe him, but the tax collectors and the prostitutes believed him, and even after you saw it you did not change your minds and believe him.

Matthew 7:21–23 (NRSV)

[21] "Not everyone who says to me, 'Lord, Lord,' will enter the kingdom of heaven, but only the one who does the will of my Father in heaven. [22] On that day many will say to me, 'Lord, Lord, did we not prophesy in your name, and cast out demons in your name, and do many mighty works in your name?' [23] Then I will declare to them, 'I never knew you; go away from me, you who behave lawlessly.'

Treasure (p. 13)

Referenced scriptures:

Matthew 6:19–21

[19] Lay not up for yourselves treasures upon earth, where moth and rust doth corrupt, and where thieves break through and steal: [20] But lay up for yourselves treasures in heaven, where neither moth nor rust doth corrupt, and where thieves do not break through nor steal: [21] For where your treasure is, there your heart will be also.

Helaman 13:35

[35] Yea, we have hid up our treasures and they have slipped away from us, because of the curse of the land.

Alas, Babylon (p. 15)

Seek (p. 17)

There are two sides to the prosperity gospel: if you're righteous you'll have worldly success, and if you have worldly success it's evidence you've been righteous. Both of these fall apart under closer examination.

We are quick to settle for proxy measures when the true goal is difficult to quantify or access. For example, it's pretty easy to measure household income, and quite difficult to nail down what constitutes "thriving." And so, in the world public policy, we end up optimizing for interventions and conditions that make people rich, when it may actually get in the way of their thriving.

In a similar way, given that it's fairly difficult to nail down your standing before God, sometimes we focus on worldly success, and convince ourselves that it correlates.

Referenced scriptures:

Jacob 2:18–19

[18] But before ye seek for riches, seek ye for the kingdom of God. [19] And after ye have obtained a hope in Christ ye shall obtain riches, if ye seek them; and ye will seek them for the intent to do good—to clothe the naked, and to feed the hungry, and to liberate the captive, and administer relief to the sick and the afflicted.

Matthew 6:31–33

[31] Therefore take no thought, saying, What shall we eat? or, What shall we drink? or, Wherewithal shall we be clothed? . . . [33] But seek ye first the kingdom of God, and his righteousness; and all these things shall be added unto you.

Amos 8:11–12

[11] Behold, the days come, saith the LORD GOD, that I will send a famine in the land, not a famine of bread, nor a thirst for water, but of hearing the words of the Lord: [12] And they shall wander from sea to sea, and from the north even to the east, they shall run to and fro to seek the word of the Lord, and shall not find it.

Lower lights (p. 18)

Once upon a time, we believed that we had inherent responsibilities to each other (Cain & Abel notwithstanding). Now, relationships are becoming increasingly commodified and depersonalized. Why do something for free—especially something difficult or uncomfortable—when instead we could bring money into the equation?

This is also related to increased loneliness, and the deterioration of local ties. In the modern era where you might live in a place for two years instead of twenty, why put in the work to get to know your neighbors? And if you don't know your neighbors, it ends up being simpler to DoorDash an order for the egg you need for a recipe than to walk next door to ask your neighbor.

"Lower lights" is a reference to the song "Let the lower lights be burning," by Philip Bliss, which also appears in the LDS hymnal.

Word of advice (p. 19)

When people talk of being "in the world, but not of the world," I most often hear them talking about avoiding sexual immorality, or political views they find unchristian, as opposed to trying to fight against the commodification of all things, and the tendency toward transactional relationships with our fellow humans and the natural world.

Referenced scriptures:

Matthew 7:6 (NIV)
> [6] Do not give dogs what is sacred; do not throw your pearls to pigs. If you do, they may trample them under their feet, and turn and tear you to pieces.

Matthew 6:6 (NIV)
> [6] But when you pray, go into your room, close the door and pray to your Father, who is unseen. Then your Father, who sees what is done in secret, will reward you.

Matthew 6:34
> [34] Take therefore no thought for the morrow: for the morrow shall take thought for the things of itself. Sufficient unto the day is the evil thereof.

We are free (p. 20)

I love the description in *Braiding Sweetgrass* (by Robin Wall Kimmerer) of humans being the "little siblings of creation," and that we have much to learn from our elder brothers and sisters, the non-human peoples. Can we learn to embody a freedom that doesn't involve theft and displacement of those who were here already?

Heavenly Home Equity Loans, Ltd. (p. 21)

This is like the prequel to the "Mortgage" poem, but here it's going a step further: you're not mortgaging your soul; you're taking a second mortgage on your heavenly treasures.

The third stanza is intentionally parallel to the temptations of Christ:

- satisfy out-of-reach desires (bread from stone)
- make evident your divine favor (cast from temple/saved by angels)
- extend your influence far beyond your dreams (kingdoms of this world)

Mint and anise and cumin (p. 23)

Referenced scriptures:

Matthew 23:23 (NRSV)
   23 Woe to you, scribes and Pharisees, hypocrites! For you tithe mint, dill, and cummin, and have neglected the weightier matters of the law: justice and mercy and faith. It is these you ought to have practiced without neglecting the others.

1 Samuel 15:22 (NRSV)
   23 Has the Lord as great delight in burnt offerings and sacrifices
      as in obedience to the voice of the LORD?
   Surely, to obey is better than sacrifice
      and to heed than the fat of rams.

Hosea 6:6 (NIV)
   6 For I desire mercy, not sacrifice, and acknowledgment of God rather than burnt offerings.

Foolish virgins (p. 24)

I love this line from a former professor: "The Bible is about bad people, and God worked with them. You're a bad person, and God will work with you."

Matthew 25:1–13 (NRSV)

¹ Then the kingdom of heaven will be like this. Ten young women took their lamps and went to meet the bridegroom. ² Five of them were foolish, and five were wise. ³ When the foolish took their lamps, they took no oil with them, ⁴ but the wise took flasks of oil with their lamps. ⁵ As the bridegroom was delayed, all of them became drowsy and slept. ⁶ But at midnight there was a shout, 'Look! Here is the bridegroom! Come out to meet him.' ⁷ Then all those young women got up and trimmed their lamps. ⁸ The foolish said to the wise, 'Give us some of your oil, for our lamps are going out.' ⁹ But the wise replied, 'No! there will not be enough for you and for us; you had better go to the dealers and buy some for yourselves.' ¹⁰ And while they went to buy it, the bridegroom came, and those who were ready went with him into the wedding banquet, and the door was shut. ¹¹ Later the other young women came also, saying, 'Lord, lord, open to us.' ¹² But he replied, 'Truly I tell you, I do not know you.' ¹³ Keep awake, therefore, for you know neither the day nor the hour.

Increase (p. 25)

In her excellent book *Short Stories By Jesus*, Amy Jill Levine emphasizes that you're not really getting full value from a parable until you've found a reading that makes you uncomfortable. This parable is typically seen as a lesson on using, and not squandering, our God-given talents and resources. I don't think that reading makes us nearly uncomfortable enough.

Nothing in this parable requires us to read the "man" as God or Christ, and while there can be fruitful readings that make such a connection, we miss valuable insight if that is the only interpretation we can find.

Referenced scriptures:

Matthew 25:14–30 (NRSV)

[14] For it is as if a man, going on a journey, summoned his slaves and entrusted his property to them; [15] to one he gave five talents, to another two, to another one, to each according to his ability. Then he went away. [16] At once the one who had received the five talents went off and traded with them and made five more talents. [17] In the same way, the one who had the two talents made two more talents. [18] But the one who had received the one talent went off and dug a hole in the ground and hid his master's money. [19] After a long time the master of those slaves came and settled accounts with them. [20] Then the one who had received the five talents came forward, bringing five more talents, saying, 'Master, you handed over to me five talents; see, I have made five more talents.' [21] His master said to him, 'Well done, good and trustworthy slave; you have been trustworthy in a few things; I will put you in charge of many things; enter into the joy of your master.' [22] And the one with the two talents also came forward, saying, 'Master, you handed over to me two talents; see, I have made two more talents.' [23] His master said to him, 'Well done, good and trustworthy slave; you have been trustworthy in a few things; I will put you in charge of many things; enter into the joy of your master.' [24] Then the one who had received the one talent also came forward, saying, 'Master, I knew that you were a harsh man, reaping where you did not sow and gathering where you did not scatter, [25] so I was afraid, and I went and hid your talent in the ground. Here you have what is yours.' [26] But his master replied, 'You wicked and lazy slave! You knew, did you, that I reap where I did not sow and gather where I did not scatter? [27] Then you ought to have invested my money with the bankers, and on my return I would have received what was my own with interest. [28] So take the talent from him, and give it to the one with the ten talents. [29] For to all those who have, more will be given, and they will have an abundance, but from those who have nothing, even what they have will be taken away. [30] As for this worthless slave, throw him

into the outer darkness, where there will be weeping and gnashing of teeth.

Alma 24:19

¹⁹ And thus we see that, when these Lamanites were brought to believe and to know the truth, they were firm, and would suffer even unto death rather than commit sin; and thus we see that they buried their weapons of peace, or they buried the weapons of war, for peace.

Luke 19:12–27 contains another, much less well-known version of this parable, which is interesting for comparison, but less relevant to this poem.

Snake in the garden (p. 27)

But really what would a post-monetary economy look like, and how tempting would it be to bring back in some inequality? The "Pride cycle" in the Book of Mormon always starts with "sorting into classes" as the first sign of downfall.

Readers with Business or Econ or Finance degrees are requested to give me grace for taking liberties with the particulars of market phenomena.

Self-reliance (p. 28)

It's always struck me as curious that the Church has a "self-reliance program"; aren't we supposed to be reliant on Christ? Should we call it "Christ Reliance"? But that wouldn't really get the right point across either, it sounds too much like "Jesus take the wheel."

If I were in charge of naming the program, I'd call it "Resilience, Resourcefulness, Reciprocity" or 3R. We're teaching people to be resilient in the face of hardship, resourceful with what they have, and as they learn these things they can enter more fully into relationships of reciprocity (with individuals and groups), which are the true key to making a community that doesn't fall apart.

I can have empathy for those who want to focus on self-reliance, especially those worn out in what I consider one of the "failure modes" of community, which we sometimes see on display in units of the Church. This is where there is a core group of "givers" that are filling all of the callings, and spending great amounts of their time in service, and a scattered periphery of "takers", some of whom have ongoing (often debilitating) needs, and some of whom just call in every couple of years with an ask ("please help me move") and otherwise don't engage. I believe one fruitful response to this involves placing a stronger emphasis on reciprocal community, in contrast to the "shepherds / sheep" duality that is the more common model. Part of this would involve doing the hard work of finding ways those traditionally on the receiving end can also give of their gifts, and participate meaningfully (and not just in a token manner) in contributing back to the community. When interacting with people interested in joining the Church, I wish we would ask them, alongside questions of faith and conversion, whether they are interested in *entering into relationship* with this community, giving of their talents as they also receive. I believe this is part of what Alma meant in his famous baptismal sermon about coming "into the fold of God," willing to "mourn with those that mourn".

Referenced scripture:

2 Nephi 4:34
> ³⁴ . . . I will not put my trust in the arm of flesh; for I know that cursed is he that putteth his trust in the arm of flesh. Yea, cursed is he that putteth his trust in man or maketh flesh his arm.

Where can I turn for peace? (p. 29)

Luke 16:1-12 (p. 31)

"Losing my job" as steward would either result from not having much money left as a result of a stock market crash, or from dying.

When trying to figure out how to behave morally in relation to money, I'm very taken with the notion of "stewardship" over that of "ownership." King Benjamin says that we are all beggars, and everything we have was not truly earned but rather gifted. In that light, deciding what to do with the funds in our care requires careful thought. (Not everyone holds this opinion; my mother tells of a comment in Sunday School where a man stated his opinion on financial morality to be "I pay my 10% and everything else is 'fun money.'")

Referenced scriptures

Luke 16:1–13 (NRSV)

[1] Then Jesus said to the disciples, "There was a rich man who had a manager, and charges were brought to him that this man was squandering his property. [2] So he summoned him and said to him, 'What is this that I hear about you? Give me an accounting of your management because you cannot be my manager any longer.' [3] Then the manager said to himself, 'What will I do, now that my master is taking the position away from me? I am not strong enough to dig, and I am ashamed to beg. [4] I have decided what to do so that, when I am dismissed as manager, people may welcome me into their homes.' [5] So, summoning his master's debtors one by one, he asked the first, 'How much do you owe my master?' [6] He answered, 'A hundred jugs of olive oil.' He said to him, 'Take your bill, sit down quickly, and make it fifty.' [7] Then he asked another, 'And how much do you owe?' He replied, 'A hundred containers of wheat.' He said to him, 'Take your bill and make it eighty.' [8] And his master commended the dishonest manager because he had acted shrewdly, for the children of this age are more shrewd in dealing with their own generation than are the children of light. [9] And I tell you, make friends for yourselves by means of dishonest wealth so that when it is gone they may welcome you into the eternal homes. [10] "Whoever is faithful in a very little is faithful also in much, and whoever is dishonest in a very little is dishonest also in much. [11] If, then, you have not been faithful with the dishonest wealth, who will entrust to you the true riches? [12] And if you have not been faithful with what belongs to another, who will give you what is your own? [13] No slave can serve two masters, for a slave will either hate the one and love the other or be devoted to the one and despise the other. You cannot serve God and wealth."

Isaiah 58:6–9 (NRSV)

⁶ Is not this the fast that I choose:
    to loose the bonds of injustice,
    to undo the straps of the yoke,
to let the oppressed go free,
    and to break every yoke?
⁷ Is it not to share your bread with the hungry
    and bring the homeless poor into your house;
when you see the naked, to cover them
    and not to hide yourself from your own kin?
⁸ Then your light shall break forth like the dawn,
    and your healing shall spring up quickly;
your vindicator shall go before you;
    the glory of the Lord shall be your rear guard.
⁹ Then you shall call, and the Lord will answer;
    you shall cry for help, and he will say, "Here I am."

Wanted: someone who deserves this coat (p. 32)

Written in the style of old newspaper want-ads.

I wrote this poem trying to distill the moral calculus involved in responding to pleas for material support.

With a certain lens (which King Benjamin espouses), none of us really "deserve" anything—it all comes from God, or a combination of the natural world and our social context.

In modern discourse, people sometimes make a distinction between the "deserving" and "undeserving" poor, where the "deserving" poor are those people who are just temporarily having a hard time, who will be grateful, and who will "pay back" into the system when they have the opportunity, or those (such as widows or orphans) who are poor "through no fault of their own." By contrast, the "undeserving" poor are ungrateful, will live off of welfare their whole lives, are just a drain on the system, etc.

But in what way does expressing gratitude impact what one "deserves?"

There's also the term "just deserts", indicating a link to "what one deserves" and "justice". So does justice dictate that those experiencing temporary hardship are owed our assistance, but those facing more permanent hardship are not?

Referenced scriptures:

Matthew 5:40 (NIV)
> [40] And if anyone wants to sue you and take your shirt, hand over your coat as well.

Luke 6:29 (NIV)
> [29] If someone slaps you on one cheek, turn to them the other also. If someone takes your coat, do not withhold your shirt from them.

See also Mosiah 4:16–24

Homework #5-40 (p. 33)

It's fun to imagine Jesus as a middle-school teacher, trying to convey his moral philosophy through short homework assignments.

Real (p. 34)

With money in banks, and payment in credit cards, if things are going well it's remarkably easy to lose track of precisely how much money you have, as long as you have "enough" of it.

In a sense, money is a fiction we all agree on (and which happens to be backed up by various national militaries). On the macro scale the "value" of a Dollar, Peso, or Yen is very much tied up with the trust that large groups of people have in the stability of the economy that it comes from. On the micro scale, because most of our money is "numbers in a computer", it's conceptually very easy to imagine those numbers getting fiddled in one direction or another.

Finally, with the stock market fluctuations, the actual "amount of money I have" can go up by hundreds in the course of a week, or thousands over the course of a couple of months, which further detaches it from "realness" in my mind.

There's also the concept of "marginal utility" and "diminishing returns"; if I have a thousand dollars, suddenly receiving another thousand dollars would represent a substantial change in my financial circumstances and purchasing power. If I have one hundred thousand dollars, adding another thousand would be much less impactful, and adding one hundred dollars might not even be noticeable.

With all that in mind, it's really weird that money is fungible such that I could, on a whim, hand over one hundred dollars of (relatively) much less meaning-filled money to someone for whom it would suddenly have tremendous meaning.

Lost (p. 35)

Amy Jill Levine points out in *Short Stories by Jesus*, the exposition on this parable given by Luke's account ("Just so, I tell you, there is joy in the presence of the angels of God over one sinner who repents") seems a little incongruous with the content of the story. The coin did not "wander off" as one could assume the lost sheep did of the adjacent parable. It was lost *by the woman*.

On a personal note, now that I have more than one kid I could totally imagine one rolling under the fridge. To be clear, I would search for them.

Referenced scriptures:

Luke 15:8–9 (NRSV)
    [8] Or what woman having ten silver coins, if she loses one of them, does not light a lamp, sweep the house, and search carefully until she finds it? [9] And when she has found it, she calls together her friends and neighbors, saying, 'Rejoice with me, for I have found the coin that I had lost.'

A Toast (p. 36)

I was raised on the 1951 movie "Scrooge," which features a song "Thank you very much" in the scene where Ebeneezer is observing the response of his neighbors to his future death. This poem has echoes of that.

Referenced scriptures:

Luke 12:16–21 (NRSV)

> [16] Then he told them a parable: "The land of a rich man produced abundantly. [17] And he thought to himself, 'What should I do, for I have no place to store my crops?' [18] Then he said, 'I will do this: I will pull down my barns and build larger ones, and there I will store all my grain and my goods. [19] And I will say to my soul, Soul, you have ample goods laid up for many years; relax, eat, drink, be merry.' [20] But God said to him, 'You fool! This very night your life is being demanded of you. And the things you have prepared, whose will they be?' [21] So it is with those who store up treasures for themselves but are not rich toward God."

The Sown (p. 37)

I'm imagining this poem as a little self-inventory, looking at the state of one's heart, and the level of hospitality that a seed might expect there.

There's an extent to which the state of one's heart is a result of one's own actions, but on the other hand: none of us invented the cares of the world, or the deceitfulness of riches, and the verse in Mark describes these "thorns" as "entering in" to choke the word.

And so we're back to dilemma of the refiner's fire—it would be nice to get rid of these thorns, but does it have to hurt quite so much?

Tuberculosis (p. 38)

The speaker is taking the quote from *Mountains Beyond Mountains* one step further—not even wanting to think about where to send money, just give it to the Church, or the Church's charity arm.

There's a version of religiosity where people find peace in the idea that "God has made the decision, so I don't have to". And another step removed: "the Prophet has determined what God has decided, so I have to neither decide nor discover what the decision was".

One way to describe my spiritual journey is peeling back those layers—first determining that the complexity of issues means I need to discover for myself the will of God, and then coming to the belief that God has such a radical commitment to agency that God wants *me* to make the decisions in many cases.

Christmas texts (p. 40)

It's so hard to know how to do community well.

Hard to know how to establish relationships that will be life-giving and humanizing instead of transactional and draining. In some cases, with this mutual aid group, we've had the same individual reach out multiple Christmases (I recognized the CashApp handle) but they didn't realize it. Not that I really begrudge it, but it definitely felt weird, and very transactional.

But it's hard to escape transactional in a society and economy that's hyper-focused on it—we can commodify anything, even people.

Referenced scripture:

Matthew 19:16
   [16] And, behold, one came and said unto him, Good Master, what good thing shall I do, that I may have eternal life?

Tornado (p. 41)

December 2021, Edwardsville Illinois.

Referenced scripture:

D&C 42:42
   [42] Thou shalt not be idle; for he that is idle shall not eat the bread nor wear the garments of the laborer.

I think about this verse so often, as a critique of rent-seeking capitalism, where those with assets can be idle because "the money works for them", and end up with more purchasing power than the laborers.

Build (p. 43)

See *We Need to Build,* by Eboo Patel.

Without them (p. 50)

See *Braiding Sweetgrass* by Robin Wall Kimmerer for a lovely exploration of our capacity for interdependence with the natural world.

"Empty chairs" is a reference to a metaphor from a song by Janice Kapp Perry which many LDS parents and grandparents draw on when they describe their hope for a heavenly scene without a single child (or grandchild) "missing" due to having failed to achieve exultation.

Referenced scriptures:

Moses 7:58

[58] And again Enoch wept and cried unto the Lord, saying: When shall the earth rest?

D&C 104:17

[17] For the earth is full, and there is enough and to spare; yea, I prepared all things, and have given unto the children of men to be agents unto themselves.

D&C 128:18

[18] . . . and behold what is that subject? It is the baptism for the dead. For we without them cannot be made perfect; neither can they without us be made perfect. Neither can they nor we be made perfect without those who have died in the gospel also . . .

Homeostasis (p. 51)

How do you measure "success" in Zion?

Referenced scriptures:

D&C 45:66–71

[66] And it shall be called the New Jerusalem, a land of peace, a city of refuge, a place of safety for the saints of the Most High God; [67] And the glory of the Lord shall be there, and the terror of the Lord also shall be there, insomuch that the wicked will not come unto it, and it shall be called Zion. [68] And it shall come to pass among the wicked,

that every man that will not take his sword against his neighbor must needs flee unto Zion for safety. [69] And there shall be gathered unto it out of every nation under heaven; and it shall be the only people that shall not be at war one with another. [70] And it shall be said among the wicked: Let us not go up to battle against Zion, for the inhabitants of Zion are terrible; wherefore we cannot stand. [71] And it shall come to pass that the righteous shall be gathered out from among all nations, and shall come to Zion, singing with songs of everlasting joy.

Dream Journal, p. 82 (p. 52)

I heard a recording of a talk while on my mission, given by some cold-war-era general authority, in which the speaker was describing the history of the Church, starting with the birth of Joseph Smith, and said something to the effect of "and as God was bringing forth Joseph Smith, the Devil was not sitting idle, because in 1818 Karl Marx was born!"

I've often thought it curious that the culture of the modern LDS church in the US has such a right-wing bent when Joseph tried a couple of times to set up a system with remarkable similarities to communism.

In this poem, I'm imagining the two of them teaming up in the afterlife to try to nudge modern change-makers away from the issues that ended up capsizing their efforts.

The Higher Law (p. 53)

In Matthew 5 Jesus uses this pattern to expand on two of the ten commandments (Thou shalt not kill, Thou shalt not commit adultery) as well as four other pieces of apparently commonly-held practice (divorce, oath swearing, retributive justice, and hating enemies).

Referenced scriptures:

Matthew 5:21–22; 27–28; 31–34; 38–39; 43–44

[21] Ye have heard that it was said by them of old time, Thou shalt not kill; and whosoever shall kill shall be in danger of the judgment:
[22] But I say unto you, That whosoever is angry with his brother

without a cause shall be in danger of the judgment: and whosoever shall say to his brother, Raca, shall be in danger of the council: but whosoever shall say, Thou fool, shall be in danger of hell fire.

27 Ye have heard that it was said by them of old time, Thou shalt not commit adultery: 28 But I say unto you, That whosoever looketh on a woman to lust after her hath committed adultery with her already in his heart.

31 It hath been said, Whosoever shall put away his wife, let him give her a writing of divorcement: 32 But I say unto you, That whosoever shall put away his wife, saving for the cause of fornication, causeth her to commit adultery: and whosoever shall marry her that is divorced committeth adultery.

33 Again, ye have heard that it hath been said by them of old time, Thou shalt not forswear thyself, but shalt perform unto the Lord thine oaths: 34 But I say unto you, Swear not at all . . .

38 Ye have heard that it hath been said, An eye for an eye, and a tooth for a tooth: 39 But I say unto you, That ye resist not evil: but whosoever shall smite thee on thy right cheek, turn to him the other also.

43 Ye have heard that it hath been said, Thou shalt love thy neighbour, and hate thine enemy. 44 But I say unto you, Love your enemies, bless them that curse you, do good to them that hate you, and pray for them which despitefully use you, and persecute you;

Psalm 24:1

1 The earth is the Lord's, and everything in it, the world, and all who live in it;

Mosiah 4:19

19 For behold, are we not all beggars? Do we not all depend upon the same Being, even God, for all the substance which we have, for both food and raiment, and for gold, and for silver, and for all the riches which we have of every kind?

Financial Laws of Zion (p. 54)

Referenced scriptures:

Ezekial 16:20–21

> [20] Moreover thou hast taken thy sons and thy daughters, whom thou hast borne unto me, and these hast thou sacrificed unto them to be devoured. Is this of thy whoredoms a small matter, [21] that thou hast slain my children, and delivered them to cause them to pass through the fire for them?

Mark 12:1–9

> [1] And he began to speak unto them by parables. A certain man planted a vineyard, and set an hedge about it, and digged a place for the winefat, and built a tower, and let it out to husbandmen, and went into a far country. [2] And at the season he sent to the husbandmen a servant, that he might receive from the husbandmen of the fruit of the vineyard. [3] And they caught him, and beat him, and sent him away empty. [4] And again he sent unto them another servant; and at him they cast stones, and wounded him in the head, and sent him away shamefully handled. [5] And again he sent another; and him they killed, and many others; beating some, and killing some. [6] Having yet therefore one son, his wellbeloved, he sent him also last unto them, saying, They will reverence my son. [7] But those husbandmen said among themselves, This is the heir; come, let us kill him, and the inheritance shall be ours. [8] And they took him, and killed him, and cast him out of the vineyard. [8] What shall therefore the lord of the vineyard do? he will come and destroy the husbandmen, and will give the vineyard unto others.

And the poor (p. 55)

Whenever I've considered setting up a utopian community, as one does, I'm struck by the difficulty of managing the financial aspect. A collective founded on wealth redistribution would obviously be much more attractive to those with little means (and indeed those with massive debt) than to those who are already well-off. One way to address this is to have participation be involuntary (i.e. instituted at a governmental level), but that's well beyond the scale of what I've contemplated.

This was a difficulty that the early church was very familiar with when experimenting with communitarian economic models, as a large proportion of the converts that emigrated to Nauvoo had very little to bring with them.

This also comes up in conflicts between missionaries and members, where missionaries find that those most receptive to their message are often those with pressing unmet temporal needs, and members would more readily welcome new people who are stable and ready to help bear the weight of running the community.

This poem is intentionally vague about the speaker's feelings about the influx of the poor to their Zion. It can be read angrily, resentfully, with resignation ("Jesus said the poor would inherit the earth, and I guess they've come to collect"), or even triumphantly ("this is a sign it's working").

Referenced scriptures:

D&C 45:66

> [66] And it shall be called the New Jerusalem, a land of peace, a city of refuge, a place of safety for the saints of the Most High God;

Moses 7:18

> [18] . . . the Lord called his people Zion, because they were of one heart and one mind, and dwelt in righteousness; and there was no poor among them.

Menial (p. 56)

"Fully automated luxury communism" is a term coined by Aaron Bastani in the mid 2010s, arguing for a future where automation reduced the need for labor, allowing all to enjoy a high standard of living.

Referenced scriptures:

Mosiah 2:14, 18

> [14] And even I, myself, have labored with mine own hands that I might serve you, and that ye should not be laden with taxes, and

that there should nothing come upon you which was grievous to be borne—and of all these things which I have spoken, ye yourselves are witnesses this day.

18 Behold, ye have called me your king; and if I, whom ye call your king, do labor to serve you, then ought not ye to labor to serve one another?

Mosiah 3:7
7 And lo, he shall suffer temptations, and pain of body, hunger, thirst, and fatigue, even more than man can suffer, except it be unto death; for behold, blood cometh from every pore, so great shall be his anguish for the wickedness and the abominations of his people.

Luke 22:44 (NRSV)
44 In his anguish he prayed more earnestly, and his sweat became like great drops of blood falling down on the ground.

Respect (p. 57)

Several of these poems are coming at the same question from different angles: What would it mean for Zion to have 'no poor among them'? Options include:

- We share resources such that poverty is "solved"
- We don't let in anyone who is poor
- We somehow reimagine poverty, as described in this poem

Referenced scripture:

Moses 7:18
18 . . . the Lord called his people Zion, because they were of one heart and one mind, and dwelt in righteousness; and there was no poor among them.

This House (p. 58)

Referenced scriptures:

D&C 109:8

> 8 Organize yourselves; prepare every needful thing, and establish a house, even a house of prayer, a house of fasting, a house of faith, a house of learning, a house of glory, a house of order, a house of God;

Matthew 5:3–11 (NRSV)

> 3 Blessed are the poor in spirit, for theirs is the kingdom of heaven.
> 4 Blessed are those who mourn, for they will be comforted.
> 5 Blessed are the meek, for they will inherit the earth.
> 6 Blessed are those who hunger and thirst for righteousness, for they will be filled.
> 7 Blessed are the merciful, for they will receive mercy.
> 8 Blessed are the pure in heart, for they will see God.
> 9 Blessed are the peacemakers, for they will be called children of God.
> 10 Blessed are those who are persecuted for the sake of righteousness, for theirs is the kingdom of heaven.
> 11 Blessed are you when people revile you and persecute you and utter all kinds of evil against you falsely on my account.

Beggar (p. 59)

At a Spiritual Directors International conference in Madison, Wisconsin, I met a woman who is living the missionary lifestyle as described in the New Testament. She is spreading the gospel, and relying on ongoing donations from the people she meets (and some from supporters back home) for her ongoing support. I was amazed at the bravery of it, and the level of trust in the body of Christ.

Need (p. 60)

My thoughts on financial matters have been greatly impacted by the writings of the anthropologist David Graeber, and especially his book *Debt: The First 5,000 Years*. In it, he describes a conception of debt from antiquity that is very different from our modern understanding. He describes small-village life, where debts are an integral part of the fabric of relationship, and the only time one would want to "settle all debts" is if they were planning to cut all ties; leaving for a faraway land, for example.

Jared Forsyth is a three-time finalist of the Mormon Lit Blitz literary competition: twice for poetry, and once for his entry "Airplanes that Crashed: A Book of Mormon Coloring Book." He enjoys talking about social issues, climbing trees, fixing things, and playing with his kids. Jared is also a maker—of poetry, bread, Islamic geometric art, websites, and wooden spoons.